How To Use Planned Ignoring (Extinction)

SECOND EDITION

R. Vance Hall
and
Marilyn L. Hall

How To Manage Behavior Series

R. Vance Hall
and
Marilyn L. Hall
Series Editors

pro·ed
An International Publisher

8700 Shoal Creek Boulevard
Austin, Texas 78757-6897
800/897-3202 Fax 800/397-7633
Order online at http://www.proedinc.com

An International Publisher
8700 Shoal Creek Boulevard
Austin, Texas 78757-6897
800/897-3202 Fax 800/397-7633
Order online at http://www.proedinc.com

Library of Congress Cataloging-in-Publication Data

Hall, R. Vance (Robert Vance), 1928–
    How to use planned ignoring (extinction) / R. Vance Hall, Marilyn
L. Hall.—2nd ed.
        p.   cm.—(How to manage behavior series)
    Includes bibliographical references.
    ISBN 0-89079-764-1 (pbk. : alk. paper)
    1. Behavior modification.   2. Extinction (Psychology).   I. Hall,
    Marilyn C.   II. Title.   III. Series
LB1060.2.H35   1998
371.39'3—dc21   97-43039
                                                                CIP

This book is designed in Palatino and Frutiger.

Production Director: Alan Grimes
Production Coordinator: Karen Swain
Managing Editor: Chris Olson
Art Director: Thomas Barkley
Designer: Lee Anne Landry
Staff Copyeditor: Suzi Hunn
Reprints Buyer: Alicia Woods
Preproduction Coordinator: Chris Anne Worsham
Project Editor: Debra Berman
Production Assistant: Dolly Fisk Jackson
Publishing Assistant: John Means Cooper

Printed in the United States of America

2   3   4   5   6   7   8   9   10   02   01   00   99

Contents

Preface to Series

The first edition of the *How To Manage Behavior Series* was launched some 15 years ago in response to a perceived need for teaching aids that could be used by therapists and trainers. The widespread demand for the series has demonstrated the need by therapists and trainers for nontechnical materials for training and treatment aids for parents, teachers, and students. Publication of this revised series includes many updated titles of the original series. In addition, several new titles have been added, largely in response to therapists and trainers who have used the series. A few titles of the original series that proved to be in less demand have been replaced. We hope the new titles will increase the usefulness of the series.

The editors are indebted to Steven Mathews, Vice President of PRO-ED, who was instrumental in the production of the revised series, as was Robert K. Hoyt, Jr. of H & H Enterprises in producing the original version.

These books are designed to teach practitioners, including parents, specific behavioral procedures to use in managing the behaviors of children, students, and other persons whose behavior may be creating disruption or interference at home, at school, or on the job. The books are nontechnical, step-by-step instructional manuals that define the procedure, provide numerous examples, and allow the reader to make oral or written responses.

The exercises in these books are designed to be used under the direction of someone (usually a professional) with a background in the behavioral principles and procedures on which the techniques are based.

The booklets in the series are similar in format but are flexible enough to be adapted to a number of different teaching situations and training environments.

As always, we invite your comments, suggestions, and questions. We are always happy to hear of your successes in changing your own behaviors and the behaviors of other persons to make your lives more pleasant, productive, and purposeful.

R. Vance Hall &
Marilyn L. Hall,
Series Editors

How To Manage Behavior Series

How To Maintain Behavior

How To Motivate Others Through Feedback

How To Negotiate a Behavioral Contract

How To Select Reinforcers

How To Teach Social Skills

How To Teach Through Modeling and Imitation

How To Use Group Contingencies

How To Use Planned Ignoring

How To Use Prompts To Initiate Behavior

How To Use Response Cost

How To Use Systematic Attention and Approval

How To Use Time-Out

Introduction

Many people, unknowingly, may strengthen and maintain unwanted behavior of others by giving attention. Parents who are unfamiliar with behavioral techniques frequently cause tantrums and crying in their children, and adults often strengthen the very behavior they would like to get rid of in other adults. They strengthen undesirable behavior by giving attention to it rather than ignoring it.

This manual provides information and exercises in the use of a technique called planned ignoring designed to decrease unwanted behavior. The exercises in this book are designed to be used under the direction of someone (usually a professional) with a background in the behavioral principles and procedures on which the planned ignoring technique is based.

Some persons will be able to begin using planned ignoring with very little assistance other than the instruction provided here. Others will need additional explanation and coaching, as well as attention and approval from someone else. Some well-established behaviors are more difficult to work with than others. For these, the assistance of a professional to provide suggestions and support is especially important. Feedback and discussion about responses to the exercises should be provided during two or more sessions. It is possible to accomplish this successfully over the telephone.

What Is Planned Ignoring?

With Young Children

Art and Sidney Gold sought professional help because both of them, especially Mrs. Gold, were becoming haggard and distraught. Their 3-year-old daughter, Judith, was keeping them awake until midnight and after. She would not go to sleep unless Mrs. Gold remained in her room. If she dropped off to sleep and her mother left her bedside, she often awoke and began crying and screaming. They had tried "letting her cry it out" but that only made the crying tantrums worse and they finally had to give in and stand by her bed and comfort her.

R. Vance Hall, PhD, is Senior Scientist Emeritus of The Bureau of Child Research and Professor Emeritus of Human Development and Family Life and Special Education at the University of Kansas. He was a pioneer in carrying out behavioral research in classrooms and in homes. Marilyn L. Hall, EdD, taught and carried out research in regular and special public school classrooms. While at the University of Kansas, she developed programs for training parents to use systematic behavior change procedures and was a successful behavior therapist specializing in child management and marriage relationships.

They took Judith to the pediatrician. His examination showed that no physical problem was causing Judith's crying.

Desperate, the parents sought professional help. Using a different strategy, they were able to put their daughter to bed and leave the room. This resulted in tantrums of increasing intensity for several nights. The tantrums and crying then subsided and within 19 days there was no more crying (based on Williams, 1959).

At School

Mike was a 15-year-old boy who had been labeled emotionally disturbed. His teacher, Mr. Garza, was at a loss about what to do with him because Mike was his most difficult student. No matter what work Mike was assigned or what he was asked to do, the request resulted in an argument or dispute. Mike would question why he should have to do the work or would claim some aspect of the assignment was not fair.

At a loss, because even the other students had begun to dislike Mike, Mr. Garza changed his approach. When Mike would begin to dispute him or argue about an assignment, he would move to help another student or begin working studiously at his desk. Within 3 weeks Mike's arguing behavior had ceased. He seemed much happier and no longer stood out as the most obnoxious student in the class. In fact, the behavior that had been primarily responsible for getting him the label emotionally disturbed had disappeared and Mike seemed far more "normal" to everyone at school, including his classmates (Hall et al., 1971).

At Home

Jim and Maxine Finley were married during the winter break of their first year in graduate school. After their marriage Maxine discovered to her annoyance that her husband was prone to swearing tantrums when they studied. Each evening she would study at the kitchen table of their small apartment while he studied at the desk in the living room. As the semester progressed, Steve's outbursts seemed to be getting more and more frequent and Maxine was increasingly concerned.

Then she changed her approach. Whereas she had been interrupting her own studies to go to Steve and ask what was bothering him, she pretended instead to be engrossed in her work. Within a few evenings, Steve's tantrums diminished and were no longer a problem. Both had more uninterrupted study time and Maxine was greatly relieved.

These three anecdotes illustrate the expected results of using planned ignoring to decrease an undesirable behavior. Even though it is common for someone to say, "He's just doing that to get attention," psychologists have increasingly recognized the importance of teaching people about planned ignoring. Persons unaware of this technique are often responsible for increasing and maintaining the negative behaviors that concern them most in those with whom they live and work.

Noticing when someone is trying to get your attention by engaging in an undesirable behavior and ignoring that behavior in a preplanned manner is planned ignoring. After reading this manual and carrying out the exercises and activities, you will see how important it is to know how to selectively use planned ignoring to decrease unwanted behaviors. You will also have begun to practice planned ignoring to bring about improved behavior in others at home, in school, and at work.

The exercises that follow will introduce you to the technique and will demonstrate how effective planned ignoring can be. The exercises help you practice planned ignoring in a conscious way, a first step in making sure you are not unknowingly maintaining behaviors you do not like in other persons.

Exercises To Demonstrate the Effects of Planned Ignoring

For you to observe how planned ignoring affects the behavior of others, choose one or more of the following exercises. Describe the results of your efforts in carrying out the exercises you have chosen.

 EXERCISE 1:   Unwanted Telephone Solicitations

You have probably wasted time and been irritated by someone trying to sell something to you over the telephone. It is often difficult to stop the person without breaking in or hanging up. If you make any comment or answer questions, the call goes on and on. The next time you receive such a call, proceed as follows:

1. As soon as you determine that the call is unwanted, say, "I'm sorry, I am really not interested."

2. If the person keeps talking, note the time.

3. From that point on, do not say anything or respond in any way (i.e., use planned ignoring).

4. Note what happens. Does the caller's pattern change?

5. Note the time the caller hangs up. If the caller tries again, use the same procedure.

(continues)

Describe what happened. _____

_____

_____

_____

Did you notice that the caller's comments between pauses were very long at first and then became increasingly shorter and shorter?   Yes ☐   No ☐

Did the person address you by name a number of times before hanging up?
Yes ☐   No ☐

Were you surprised at how long it took for the person to hang up?
Yes ☐   No ☐

Was it hard for you to not say something as the person talked on?
Yes ☐   No ☐

What do you think would happen if everyone responded to such calls with planned ignoring, or if everyone refused to buy products advertised in tasteless television commercials?

EXERCISE 2:   The Effects of Planned Ignoring on Someone Who Interrupts

Observe one of your own children, a student in your classroom, a friend, or a coworker who has the habit of interrupting you while you are saying or doing something. The next time this happens, try not to pay attention to the interruption. If you feel you must speak, say, "I'm sorry, I'm busy," or whatever is appropriate. Then, no matter what the person does, ignore him or her. Keep track of the number of times the person tries to interrupt you.

Describe what happened. _____

_____

_____

Did the person try repeatedly to interrupt you?   Yes ☐   No ☐
How many times or for how long did the person try to interrupt before he or she quit or you gave in? _____

(*continues*)

Did the person show anger or irritation at you when you did not respond?
Yes ☐   No ☐   If so, in what way?

_____

_____

_____

_____

Was if difficult for you not to respond to the person in this situation?
Yes ☐   No ☐

EXERCISE 3:   The Effects of Planned Ignoring on Conversation

Pick someone you see rather frequently who is in the habit of complaining,
gossiping, or bad-mouthing someone else. The next time this happens, ignore
the comments by not responding to them. If necessary:

1. Switch the topic of conversation or say something like, "He/She always
   speaks highly of you."
2. Become very busy doing something else.
3. Walk away from the person.

If the person changes the subject and begins talking about something else:

1. Listen attentively.
2. Smile.
3. Ask questions or comment about the new topic.

Describe what happened. _____

_____

_____

_____

(continues)

Did the person try to return to the habitual talk?   Yes ☐   No ☐

Were you able to keep from responding?   Yes ☐   No ☐
If yes, was the content of your conversation different from usual?
Yes ☐   No ☐

Were you surprised at the results?   Yes ☐   No ☐

Defining Planned Ignoring

Having read the introduction to this manual and having observed the effects of your attention on the behavior of others in carrying out the exercises, you should have a good understanding of planned ignoring, or the practice of deliberately setting out to decrease an undesirable behavior by completely ignoring it.

In your own words, describe what planned ignoring is and what it does.

What it is: _____

_____

What it does: _____

_____

You're right if you said it is the procedure of ignoring behavior in an effort to cause it to decrease.

Can you think of a time when you have observed an event in which planned ignoring decreased an inappropriate behavior? Describe it.

_____

_____

_____

_____

(continues)

Describe an event you have experienced or observed in which someone could or should have used planned ignoring to decrease a behavior, but didn't.

_____

_____

_____

Now that we have defined and given examples of planned ignoring, it seems to be a very simple and commonsense procedure. Nevertheless, it is often very difficult to begin using it to decrease behavior. In fact, you may have found it difficult to carry out the exercises above.

This is because many people already have well-established habits of attending to behavior that really should be ignored, especially with certain people in certain situations (e.g., when children tantrum in the presence of company). Another reason is that people do not know what to expect when they first start using planned ignoring and they may stop before they really have a chance to make it work. Even worse, if that happens, they may make the behavior worse rather than better.

You now know what is meant by planned ignoring and understand its effects on behavior. You are ready to learn the eight basic steps for using planned ignoring to decrease an undesirable behavior in someone you know or with whom you work.

Even though you think you understand the basic principle of using planned ignoring, you should follow through on each of these eight steps. If you do, your chances of being successful with this important skill on your first try are greatly increased.

Basic Steps in Using Planned Ignoring

▶ **Step 1: Define or pinpoint the behavior you want to change.**

The first step in using planned ignoring is to decide exactly what behavior(s) to change. Because the procedure is designed to decrease behavior, it is necessary to pinpoint a behavior you do not want. This is usually not too difficult because in our society we tend to focus on behaviors that irritate and annoy us rather than noticing desirable behaviors. We must also think about behavior we want to maintain, as well as the behavior we want to decrease.

A good definition of the behavior we want to change through planned ignoring will answer the following questions: Who? What? When? and

Where?—that is, whose behavior is being pinpointed, exactly what the behavior is, and when and where it takes place.

Ms. Williams was a first-year, fifth-grade teacher who was exasperated at one of her students, Glenn. Each time she looked up from her desk, Glenn was at her elbow asking questions about the assignment, wanting to know if his work was right, or wanting to tell her something irrelevant. Ms. Williams liked Glenn. He was a good student and he had a charming way about him. She knew he liked her; in fact, she suspected that was one reason he so frequently came to her desk. That was also one reason she found it difficult to reprimand him, though she had asked him a number of times not to come to her desk without permission. His behavior was becoming increasingly annoying, however, and she felt she must do something.

When asked to define the behavior she wished to change, Ms. Williams had little difficulty deciding that it was the number of times that Glenn appeared at her desk without permission that was of concern to her. She decided that it was acceptable if he came to her desk after raising his hand and receiving permission. She defined the unwanted behavior as any occasion while class was in session that Glenn came within 3 feet of her desk to ask a question, show his work, make a comment, or otherwise make contact with her without first obtaining permission.

It was a good definition because it answered the who, what, when, and where questions. Glenn was who, any occasion Glenn came within 3 feet of her desk to contact her without having first obtained permission was what and where, and during class time was when.

Practice in Pinpointing

In the situation below, pinpoint a behavior that might be a target for planned ignoring.

Newspaper editor Clyde Adams has a problem with his top reporter, Julie Clark. Although Julie's reporting is outstanding, several things she does irritate Clyde and cause friction among the other staff. Every day just as the newspaper deadline approaches, Julie enters Clyde's office and goes into detail about the contacts she has made and the stories she has written that day. These sessions last 5 or 10 minutes and keep Clyde from his work. At the weekly staff meetings, Julie tries to dominate the discussions. She uses the occasions to brag about her own writing techniques and makes comments about any suggestions made by other members of the reporting staff. If someone comes up with an idea, in a short time, Clyde finds that he and Julie are discussing it as if it had really come from Julie. Finally, Clyde finds he is spending an increasing amount of time listening to Julie's complaints about the inadequacies of other employees, about problems in the press room, and about other matters that should not be her concerns. Clyde has determined there is little foundation to most of these complaints.

Describe a behavior Clyde might pinpoint and set out to change.

Who? _____

What? _____

Where? _____

When? _____

Did you focus on a specific inappropriate behavior Clyde might decrease?
Yes ☐   No ☐

If you were able to check yes, good. It is usually better to focus on one
behavior at a time. If you tried to include more than one specific behavior,
try again. Did you answer the questions who, what, where, and when?
Yes ☐   No ☐

*In defining a target behavior, avoid using labels. Sometimes people use the terms
"hostility," "laziness," "ego," "attitudes," and other labels to describe behaviors
about which they are concerned. If you thought about using such a label in the example above, try instead to focus on a specific behavior. Such labels are usually too broad
and can mean too many different things to different persons.*

Describe how you would pinpoint a behavior you would like to change using
planned ignoring. (Try to choose a simple but important one with which you
think you will have success on your first try.)

Who? _____

What? _____

Where? _____

When? _____

(continues)

Check your answer with the person working with you on this problem. If you both agree that the definition is a good one, make a check here ☐. If not, work on your definition in the space provided below until you can put a check in the box.

_____

_____

_____

_____

▶ **Step 2: Measure the behavior selected.**

The second step is to get an idea about the level of the behavior you want to change. This is important for three reasons:

1. You may find that the behavior you wish to change is not as much of a problem as you thought. If that happens, so much the better. Then the thing to do is define another behavior to decrease using planned ignoring.

2. Measuring the behavior before and after you begin planned ignoring will provide feedback and help you to see whether there really is a change in the behavior. This is particularly important because it is very likely that when you use planned ignoring the behavior will get worse before it gets better. If you expect this and observe the change, it will help you to continue using planned ignoring until you are successful.

3. If you measure the behavior and note improvement, it will be easier to remember to give attention to the desired behavior you observe. Planned ignoring will not work unless you also remember to attend to the behaviors you do want.

Counting Behaviors

There are several ways to measure behavior. The most appropriate measurement technique may be to count each incidence of the behavior as it happens. Such behaviors might include hits, tantrums, crying, arguments, and name calling. In most cases this can be done by keeping a tally with paper and pencil each time the behavior occurs. That is what Ms. Williams did in counting the number of times Glenn came to her desk without permission each day. Each time he came to her desk, she made a tally on a sheet of paper she had prepared for that purpose. At the end of the school day, it was easy for her to see how many times he had been at her desk. This is what her record looked like:

Mon	Tues	Wed	Thurs	Fri
III	ꟿ I	IIII	ꟿ	ꟿ II

Thus she knew that in the 5 days of that week, Glenn had visited her desk 3, 6, 4, 5, and 7 times, for a total of 25 times or an average of 5 times a day.

Timing Behaviors

Some behaviors that may be of concern to you and that can be measured by counting can also be measured in terms of time. In some cases, knowing how long behaviors last may be more important than how many times they occur. For example, a parent may get a better idea of the level of bedtime tantrums by clocking how long they last rather than how many there are. Each evening a child may have only one tantrum but it may vary from 1 to 45 minutes. Behaviors can be timed using a stopwatch, but keeping track on a wristwatch or kitchen clock is usually accurate enough to get a good estimate of how long a behavior lasts.

In the example below, an employer kept track of how many minutes a certain employee spent talking to him each day about trivial matters. He did this by noting the time such conversations began and when they ended and totaling the time at the end of each workday.

Mon	Tue	Wed	Thurs	Fri
10:20 to 10:45 = 25	10:10 to 10:17 = 7	10:15 to 10:20 = 5	9:00 to 9:14 = 14	9:10 to 9:19 = 9
1:04 to 1:14 = 10	1:15 to 1:31 = 16	3:30 to 3:42 = 12	11:05 to 11:25 = 20	1:30 1:41 = 11
	3:20 to 3:50 = 30			
35 min	53 min	17 min	34 min	20 min

Most behaviors that lend themselves to control by planned ignoring can be measured by counting or timing. Additional information on how to define and measure behavior is available in Hall and Van Houten (1983).

Describe how you will measure the level of the behavior you plan to change in order to see what its level is and whether or not planned ignoring is having an effect. Remember, it is important to get an idea of the level of the behavior before you try to change it.

_____

_____

_____

If your instructor agrees that the method you have chosen is a good one, put a check here ☐. If there is a question about your measurement procedure, work on it until you can put a check in the box.

Recording the Behavior

Although you may be keeping a record of the behavior selected on a piece of paper, a calendar, or somewhere else, also record it in the space below so that your instructor can easily understand your record:

	Day or Session									
	1	2	3	4	5	6	7	8	9	10
Level of Behavior										

Keep recording the behavior long enough to feel certain you have a measure of its average level. When you have enough information about the behavior, define the average level:

On the average, the behavior occurs about _____

_____

Charting Behavior

Many persons find it helpful and informative to create a visual picture of the level of a behavior by putting it on a graph. For example, Ms. Williams, who counted the number of times a day Glenn came to her desk without permission, made the following graph (baseline record):

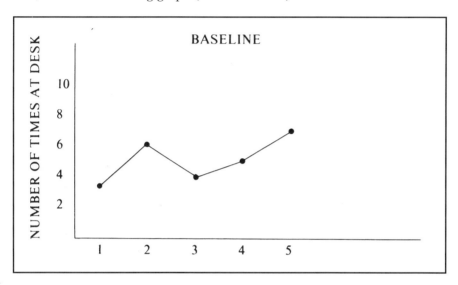

The employer who made a record of the number of minutes a worker spent talking to him made the following graph (baseline record):

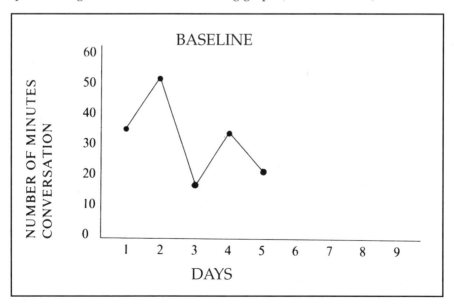

EXERCISE: Charting Behavior (optional)

In the back of this manual is a sample raw data sheet that many persons use to create a visual display of the target behavior. You may want to use that form to display the behavior you have chosen to change. The vertical axis shows the level of the behavior. Days or sessions are recorded across the horizontal axis.

Chart the behavior you have measured by using a data point for each observation session. This record of the behavior before you try to change it is called a baseline. Ask your instructor to help you chart it if you are uncertain about how to do it. (Further discussion of measuring and charting behavior may be found in Hall & Van Houten, 1983.)

▶ **Step 3: Set a goal for the target behavior.**

Once you have measured the level of the behavior you want to change, it is advisable to set a goal. For example, the employer who made a record of the number of minutes an employee spent talking to him decided that an adequate goal would be to have the employee decrease the talking to no more than 5 minutes per day.

Indicate here what the target level of the behavior you have chosen should be.

_____

_____

_____

_____

▶ **Step 4: Decide what kind of planned ignoring to use.**

After you have defined the behavior to be decreased and measured its present level, you are ready to begin using planned ignoring. There are several things to consider at this step:

1. Once you begin using planned ignoring, you must use it consistently or your efforts will fail. If you fail, your attempt at planned ignoring may even be detrimental to the person.

2. The behavior you select to decrease may get worse before it gets better, and you should be prepared for this occurrence.

3. The person whose behavior you plan to ignore may engage in some form of aggressive behavior when you begin using planned ignoring.

4. It is more difficult to carry out planned ignoring under some circumstances than others, and you need to be aware of possible problems before you begin your particular exercise.

5. There are several forms of planned ignoring, and you should select one you can carry out effectively.

6. It may be necessary for you to get support and feedback from someone else to help you to stick to your planned ignoring program.

7. At the same time you are ignoring the behavior you wish to decrease, it is important to give attention to other behaviors you want to maintain.

Mr. and Mrs. Croker were at a loss as to what to do about their 4-year-old son, John. John had developed a terrible temper and displayed it more and more frequently as he grew older. John's parents had tried reasoning with him. On occasion they had tried not giving in to his tantrums, but that only seemed to make them worse. They had taken him to a pediatrician but he could find no physical basis for John's demanding behavior. For the most part his parents avoided John's tantrums by letting him have his own way. Mrs. Croker had become especially adept at anticipating John's wants. Of late, however, John's demands had become so unreasonable that the Crokers had begun to resent their son. Mr. Croker had resorted to spanking him on several occasions but that led to even more violent outbursts. The Crokers had noticed that John was more inclined to have tantrums when they were in public places or when company was present. They felt helpless in these situations. They were seldom invited into others' homes and even relatives rarely came to see them.

Finally the Crokers sought professional help. The psychologist they contacted, Dr. Lee, suggested that they use planned ignoring to reduce tantrum behavior. Before they began, however, she prepared them for what they could expect.

After Dr. Lee had them define what they meant by tantrum behavior, the Crokers measured the level of tantrums. They were somewhat surprised that tantrums occurred at the rate of only five or six a week, which meant less than one a day. They also noted that these tantrums lasted only 3 to 5 minutes on the average. However, they realized that even this level was too high and that they had become skilled in avoiding tantrums. Otherwise they were certain the level would be much higher. They said they felt that an acceptable level would be one tantrum per week.

Expect the Behavior To Increase

In helping the Crokers plan how to use planned ignoring, Dr. Lee told them that the first thing to expect would be an increase in tantrums. She explained that tantrums would probably get more frequent and last longer than ever before. This is because when tantrums start they usually do not amount to much, perhaps a few tears. However, if the parents attend to the tears and give in, the next time the child wants something, more tears can be expected. If, at some point, the parents decide not to give in, the child is liable to cry a little longer and louder, perhaps holding his or her breath or kicking and yelling. If this results in the child's having his or her way, the child, in a sense, learns to have even more violent tantrums. If a little tantrum does not work, the child learns to throw a bigger one. When someone begins ignoring behavior previously not ignored (i.e., given attention), the first thing that happens is that the behavior gets stronger.

Dr. Lee told them that is one of the main reasons for recording a behavior prior to using planned ignoring. She said, "It will help you to stick by the program if the behavior begins to increase at first. If you expect it and record and graph it, it is easier to stick to the planned ignoring."

In John's case, here is what happened during the first few days.

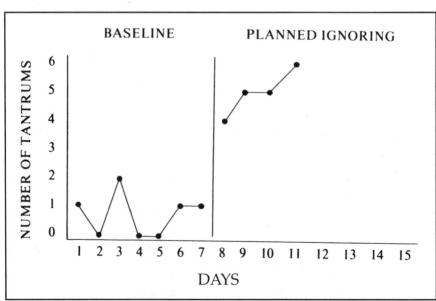

Not only did the number of John's tantrums increase, but so did their length and severity. In fact, Mr. Croker timed one tantrum on the third day that lasted 1 hour, 48 minutes. Both parents thought it would never end. Mrs. Croker said, "By golly, it is getting worse, just as we were told it would, but we know if we hold out it will soon get better."

Aggressive Behavior May Occur

Another thing the Crokers were told to expect was that John might very well engage in some aggressive behavior. Because *aggressive* is a general term, Dr. Lee explained that what the Crokers really needed to expect was that John might yell, curse, even hit or kick and throw things. This is much like what happens when someone puts money in a vending machine. If nothing comes out, usually one of the first things the person does is to pound or even kick the machine. Forewarned, the Crokers were prepared when John shouted, "I hate you," at his parents and began trying to kick his mother. As planned, when this happened, his mother left the room and locked herself in the bedroom until the tantrum subsided.

Attending to Appropriate Behavior

Dr. Lee explained that, while they were using planned ignoring for John's tantrums, it was also important to give attention and approval when he responded appropriately. "In effect," she stated, "you are taking attention from the behavior you do not want. In its place you need to give attention for the behavior you do want." She cautioned them to be alert to the times when John was asked to do something or when they had to tell him, "No," and he did not have a tantrum. In the beginning she encouraged them to tell him how pleased they were with his behavior when he had gone for a time without a tantrum or had not had a tantrum in a situation that would previously have caused a tantrum.

▶ **Step 5: Rehearse planned ignoring.**

In order for them to be surer of themselves, Dr. Lee suggested that the three of them try role-playing several situations they might face with John. She set this up in the following way: Mrs. Croker was assigned the role of John, Mr. Croker was assigned the role of himself, and Dr. Lee was the recorder. The Crokers then played the scene.

John (age 4): Your father has just read a book to you. Now you want him to play a game. You get the game and beg him to play. When he refuses because he wants to read the paper, you cry, holler, demand, kick, and stamp your feet.

Mr. Croker: You have just given John 15 minutes of your evening. You tell John that you are going to read the paper now and that tomorrow evening you will play Chutes and Ladders. Then you ignore his further demands no matter how wild he becomes.

The recorder, Dr. Lee, guided the parents through all the steps and gave feedback about how well Mr. Croker used the planned ignoring components listed on the recording sheet.

Role-Playing Recording Sheet

The role-playing recording sheet was checked as all three persons, Mr. Croker, Dr. Lee, and Mrs. Croker, played the part of John's father.

Sample Recording Sheet: Role-Playing Planned Ignoring

Parent Behavior	Person Playing Planned Ignorer (Parent)		
	Mr. Croker	Dr. Lee	Mrs. Croker
1. Look away from child	✔	✔	✔
2. Move away from child (at least 3 feet)	✔	✔	✔
3. Maintain impassive face	✔	O	✔
4. Ignore all requests	✔	✔	✔
5. If necessary, leave room	✔	✔	✔
6. Begin ignoring within 5 seconds	O	✔	✔

Dr. Lee recorded that Mr. Croker did a good job of carrying out the planned ignoring procedures; however, he waited too long to begin them. That is, he listened and looked at John longer than 5 seconds after John began begging because his father refused his request.

Then they switched roles. Dr. Lee played Mr. Croker, Mr. Croker played John, and Mrs. Croker was the recorder. Dr. Lee could not resist a smile at one of John's (Mr. Croker's) tantrum behaviors and so missed a point on that account.

Then they switched roles again, with Mrs. Croker playing her husband, Dr. Lee playing John, and Mr. Croker acting as the recorder. Mrs. Croker did well.

Planned Ignoring Procedures

With the help of Dr. Lee, the Crokers made a list of several ways to carry out planned ignoring:

1. Refuse to speak to or answer John when he is in a tantrum.

2. Look away as long as John is in a tantrum (break eye contact).

3. Turn back on John.

4. Walk away from John.

5. Go into another room and close the door.

6. Go outside or, if outside, go inside the house.

7. If in a public place, walk away or go to the car (keeping a covert eye on John to be sure he is safe).

8. If friends or relatives are present, seek their cooperation in advance and ask them to use planned ignoring.

Being Consistent Once You Begin

Before the Crokers were through, they used all of the procedures listed. It was especially difficult for them on the occasions when John had a tantrum in public and when company was present. However, they decided it was better to put up with the stares and comments over the short term than to be forced to continue putting up with John's tantrums.

They were surprised when some of their friends voiced approval. Knowing they were using planned ignoring to help John and that it was best for him also gave them determination. The record they kept also gave them confidence, especially when, on the 12th day, the number and intensity of tantrums began to decrease. From then on, as Dr. Lee had predicted, tantrums decreased and soon stopped. The Crokers were delighted. After a few weeks there were no tantrums, which was even better than the original goal of one tantrum per week. John had become much more cheerful and seemed happier then he ever had before. The parents found themselves really enjoying him for the first time since he had been a baby. The chart that follows is a record of John's tantrums during the baseline and the first 13 days of planned ignoring.

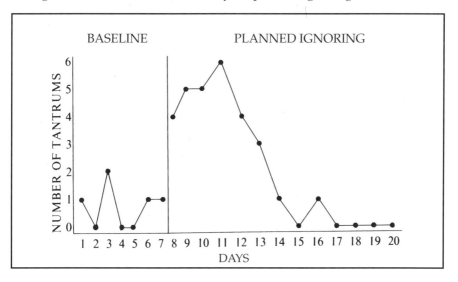

▶ Step 6: Select what procedures to use.

In the case of John Croker, the parents planned in advance the specific things they would do. In making your own plans, list the ways you plan to carry out your planned ignoring program.

1. _____

2. _____

3. _____

4. _____

5. _____

6. _____

7. _____

You probably should have listed, at the least, *look away, maintain an impassive face, do not answer,* and *move away within 5 seconds.* Check with your instructor, and if he or she agrees with your list, put a check here ☐.

Your instructor, your spouse, or another person should help you set up a role-playing situation to practice before you begin. In doing so, one should play the person whose behavior is to be decreased, one the role of the planned ignorer, and one the recorder. Each should shift roles so that the group goes through the exercise three times, once with each person in each position.

Scene: Set the scene describing the roles of

Target person: _____

_____

_____

_____

_____

(continues)

Planned ignorer: _____

_____

_____

_____

_____

Recorder: Will guide the role-playing and give feedback.

Recording Sheet: List behaviors to be checked.

Recording Sheet: Role-Playing Planned Ignoring

| | Person Playing Planned Ignorer (Parent) | | |
| | 1 | 2 | 3 |
Parent Behavior	___	___	___
1. Look away from child			
2. Move away from child (at least 3 feet)			
3. Maintain impassive face			
4. Ignore all requests			
5. If necessary, leave room			
6. Begin ignoring within 5 seconds			

Giving Attention to the Behavior You Do Want

Planned ignoring will work best if you ignore unwanted behavior while you give attention and approval to the behavior you do want.

List some of the behaviors you will look for and give attention to by looking at, talking to, smiling, coming close to, and perhaps even touching the person when the behaviors occur.

(continues)

1. _____

2. _____

3. _____

4. _____

5. _____

When To Use Planned Ignoring

It should now be clear to you how often you should use planned ignoring once you decide to begin using it and how soon planned ignoring should begin once you observe the behavior you wish to decrease.

1. When should you use planned ignoring once you have decided to do it?

_____

2. How soon after the behavior starts should you begin? _____ seconds.

If you said every time the behavior occurs, and that you should begin within 5 seconds, you are correct.

▶ **Step 7: Review.**

You now know the basic steps for using planned ignoring in a systematic way to decrease a behavior you have selected.

Summarize the information from the first six steps.

1. Define or pinpoint the behavior. Describe the behavior you will change.

(continues)

Who? _____

What? _____

When? _____

Where? _____

2. Measure the behavior.

Describe the current level of the behavior you have measured. _____

_____

3. Select a goal for the target behavior.

Indicate the goal you have selected for the target behavior. _____

_____

_____

4. Select the kind of planned ignoring to use.

Describe the planned ignoring procedures you are going to use. _____

_____

_____

5. Rehearse planned ignoring.

Did you rehearse your planned ignoring procedure?   Yes ☐   No ☐

6. Determine when to act.

Describe when you will begin using planned ignoring. _____

_____

_____

_____

_____

(continues)

7. Give attention to desirable behavior.

List behaviors you do want that you will give attention to. _____

_____

_____

_____

8. Anticipate potential problems.

List what is liable to happen to the behavior when you first begin using planned ignoring.

_____

_____

_____

What should happen if you continue with planned ignoring? _____

_____

_____

What will you do if the person makes a scene when others are present?

_____

_____

_____

▶ **Step 8: Implement your program.**

If you have gone through this manual and carried out the exercises and reader activities, you should be prepared to begin using planned ignoring. But before you begin, consider one more very important point that has to do with making your intentions clear to the person whose behavior you are going to change.

When the person whose behavior you want to change first begins to engage in the undesirable behavior, you should identify the behavior to him and state that you plan to ignore it. You should state your intention only once, do it in a matter-of-fact tone, and then make certain you do ignore the behavior from then on. For example, you might say, "I'm sorry, I will not discuss it further," or "I plan to ignore that behavior from now on," or "That is something I do not care to talk about; let's change the subject."

The advantage of stating your intention, if you do indeed then begin planned ignoring, is that it makes clear to the person what behavior is causing the planned ignoring. If you then stick to your intention, the person learns that, when you say you are not going to attend to a behavior, it is useless to argue, fuss, or pursue that subject, and the person will begin to engage in more appropriate behavior. Thus, you make a commitment to the course of action you have chosen—planned ignoring—and once you make that statement, it helps you carry out your resolve and not attend to the behavior that is causing the difficulty.

Another advantage is that, if you clearly identify the behavior you are going to ignore, the person will realize you are not ignoring him or her but rather you are ignoring a particular behavior. The person can quickly see that all he or she needs to do to gain your attention again is to stop that behavior and your relationship will resume. That is why stating your intention to ignore a particular behavior can be a matter of courtesy that makes your planned ignoring more acceptable and more effective than if you merely ignore some behavior without identifying it for the person who is engaging in the behavior.

That is not to say that planned ignoring will not work without explanation. In fact, in some social situations, it may be more courteous simply not to respond than to define what it is you have decided to ignore.

Indicate here whether the behavior you plan to ignore is one that lends itself to stating your intentions beforehand (one time only).   Yes ☐   No ☐

If yes, what statement will you make? _____

_____

_____

_____

▶ **Step 9: Evalute the results.**

_____

It is important to continue observing the behavior you measured to see if there is a change in the level. Be prepared to record the results of your efforts during the first week or so of observation.

	Day or Session									
	1	2	3	4	5	6	7	8	9	10
Level of Behavior										

How does this level compare with the average level before you began using planned ignoring? An increase? ☐   A decrease? ☐   No change? ☐

How did the person seem to respond? _____

Was there an initial increase in undesired behavior? _____

_____

_____

When did you first notice a decrease in the behavior you were ignoring?

_____

_____

_____

What was the most difficult thing about sticking to your program of planned ignoring?

_____

_____

_____

(continues)

Do you have another behavior you are ready to try to change using planned ignoring?   Yes ☐   No ☐   If yes, what is it?

Who? _____

What? _____

When? _____

Where? _____

Charting Behavior Exercise (optional)

If you made a graph of the person's behavior before using planned ignoring, draw a vertical line on your chart and continue to record the level of the behavior, as Mr. and Mrs. Croker did in graphing John's tantrums (see page 19). This will give you a visual record of the behavior selected so that it will be easy to see if it goes up and then decreases.

What To Do If Planned Ignoring Does Not Work

Although planned ignoring is effective in most cases, occasionally one encounters conditions in which it cannot be used. For example, some children are so skilled in throwing tantrums and forcing people to attend to them that to ignore them may be impossible. This situation arises when the behavior endangers them or others or may cause significant property damage. Behaviors such as running away from home or breaking the law usually do not lend themselves to planned ignoring. Children sometimes break windows or do other dangerous acts that are all but impossible to ignore. Although few go to such extremes, one must be aware of such possibilities and have a plan of action. In such cases, a time-out or response cost procedure may be appropriate (see *How To Use Time-Out*, Hall & Hall, 1998, and *How To Use Response Cost*, Thibadeau, 1998).

Sometimes inappropriate behavior is maintained by the attention received from others. In such cases it will be necessary to enlist the cooperation of those others if planned ignoring is to be successful. For example, if a teacher chooses to ignore noises being made by a student in the classroom, chances are the noises will stop, especially if the teacher attends to the student when he or she does not make noise. However, if the student's classmates giggle and point, this attention may maintain the noisy behavior. In such cases the teacher will need to enlist the cooperation of the other students or perhaps institute another procedure. Many teachers have been successful in enlisting the assistance of classmates for improved behavior on the part of the student (Hall & Copeland, 1972).

Where To From Here?

This book has explained how to use planned ignoring to decrease undesirable behavior. It is a basic procedure that everyone should understand and be able to use. Without understanding, however, it is possible to misuse planned ignoring and unwittingly increase and maintain the undesired behaviors.

The examples were simple and straightforward. All are based on actual case histories and are representative of behaviors that can be managed with planned ignoring. The list of behaviors that can be decreased using this technique is almost without limit. As has been pointed out, however, some behaviors in some persons and situations will be difficult or impossible to deal with using planned ignoring alone. However, even with these behaviors, planned ignoring used in conjunction with other procedures will probably be effective.

If planned ignoring does prove to be inappropriate or ineffective, other procedures such as time-out, contingency contracting, systematic reinforcement, response cost, positive practice, or a token system may be indicated. With most behaviors, however, planned ignoring, along with its companion procedure of systematic attention and approval, should probably be tried before resorting to more expensive and restrictive procedures. Planned ignoring, if properly implemented, has the advantages of being inexpensive and not requiring materials or equipment. In the long run it is easy to apply and has long-lasting results, even though in the beginning it may be difficult to adhere to.

Persons who learn to use planned ignoring and to recognize how effective it can be in decreasing undesirable behavior will soon begin to incorporate it in their own style of interaction with others. Very quickly it will become a part of the person's way of dealing with situations, not as a bag of tricks, but as an integral part of the person's style.

Good teachers spend most of their time attending to the appropriate behavior of their students, encouraging them for their efforts. Effective parents notice the good behavior of their children and let them know they are proud of how well they are doing. Successful husbands and wives notice and comment on the many things their spouses do to help and please them. Effective employers let their employees know when their work performance is good.

Persons skilled in planned ignoring do not attend primarily to the negative behaviors they see because, if they do give attention to the behaviors they do not want, they very likely will increase them. Most persons would rather get attention for something than be ignored. That is why they engage in the behaviors that bring them attention. People who understand this basic principle use planned ignoring. Rather than being controlled by the person who gains attention with inappropriate behavior, you refuse to give your attention. By withdrawing attention for that undesirable behavior and then giving it to more appropriate behavior, a more healthy and pleasant relationship develops.

That is the secret and the promise of planned ignoring. It is a fundamental skill that nurtures good interaction with persons you know and love, at home, in school, and on the job.

Program Follow-up

This section should be reviewed and filled out 2 weeks or more after you have initiated your program. It will provide feedback to you and your instructor on how well planned ignoring has worked for you.

1. Was your first attempt successful?   Yes ☐   No ☐

2. What changes in behavior did you observe? _____

3. What problems did you encounter? _____

_____

_____

_____

4. Were you able to solve these problems? If so, how? _____

_____

_____

_____

(continues)

5. Describe briefly any other behavior you have changed. _____

_____

_____

_____

6. Do you plan to continue using planned ignoring?   Yes ☐   No ☐

   With whom? _____

7. Is planned ignoring a skill you think you now understand and can use effectively?   Yes ☐   No ☐   Maybe ☐

8. Comments: _____

_____

_____

_____

LEVEL OF BEHAVIOR

Subject(s): _____

Setting: _____

Behavior Management

RAW DATA SHEET

Author: _____

Title: _____

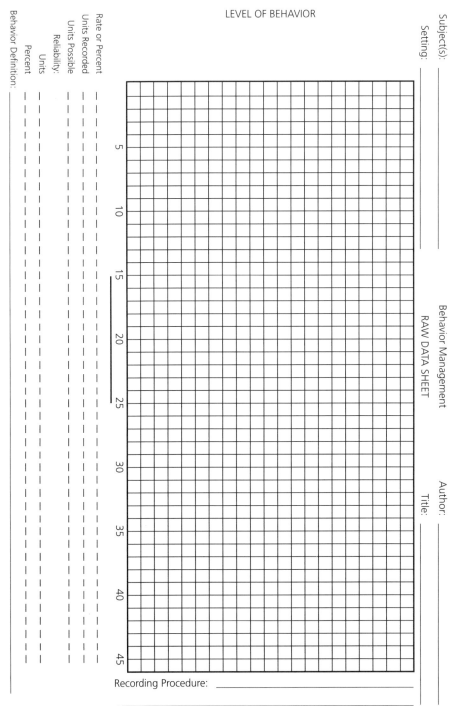

Behavior Definition: _____

Percent _ _

Units _ _

Reliability: _ _ _

Units Possible _ _ _

Units Recorded _ _ _

Rate or Percent _ _ _

Recording Procedure: _____

References and Further Reading

Axelrod, S. (1983). *Behavior modification for the classroom teacher.* New York: McGraw-Hill.

Craighead, W. E., Kazdin, A. E., & Mahoney, M. J. (1981). *Behavior modification: principles, issues and applications.* Boston: Houghton-Mifflin.

Hall, R. V., & Van Houten, R. (1983). *Managing behavior: Part 1. The measurement of behavior.* Austin, TX: PRO-ED.

Hall, R. V. (1975). *Managing behavior: Part 2. Basic principles.* Austin, TX: PRO-ED.

Hall, R. V., Axelrod, S., Tyler, L., Grief, E., Jones, F. C., & Robertson, R. (1972). Modification of behavior problems in the home with a parent as observer and experimenter. *Journal of Applied Behavior Analysis, 5,* 53–64.

Hall, R. V., & Copeland, R. (1972). The responsive teaching model: A first step in shaping school personnel as behavior modification specialists. In *Proceedings of the Third Banff International Conference on Behavior Modification* (pp. 125–150). Champaign, IL: Research Press.

Hall, R. V., Fox, R., Willard, D., Goldsmith, L., Emerson, M., Owen, M., Davis, F., & Porcia, E. (1971). The teacher as observer and experimenter in the modification of disputing and talking-out behaviors. *Journal of Applied Analysis, 4,* 141–149.

Hall, R. V., & Hall, M. C. (1998). *How to use time-out.* Austin, TX: PRO-ED.

Hall, R. V., Lund, D., & Jackson, D. (1968). Effects of teacher attention on study behavior. *Journal of Applied Behavior Analysis, 1,* 1–12.

Hall, R. V., & Van Houten, R. (1983). *Managing behavior: Part I. Measurement of behavior.* Austin, TX: PRO-ED.

Harris, F. R., Johnston, M. K., Kelly, C. S., & Wolf, M. M. (1964). Effects of positive social reinforcement on regressed crawling of a nursery school child. *Journal of Educational Psychology, 55,* 35–41.

Kazdin, A. E. (1994). *Behavior modification in applied settings.* Pacific Grove, CA: Brooks/Cole.

Miller, L. K. (1997). *Principles of everyday behavior analysis.* Pacific Grove, CA: Brooks/Cole.

Rusch, F. R., Rose, T., & Greenwood, C. R. (1988). *Behavior analysis in special education.* Englewood Cliffs, NJ: Prentice-Hall.

Sulzer-Azeroff, B., & Mayer, G. R. (1991). *Behavior analysis for lasting change.* Fort Worth, TX: Holt, Rinehart and Winston.

Thibadeau, S. F. (1998). *How to use response cost.* Austin, TX: PRO-ED.

Williams, C. D. (1959). The elimination of tantrum behavior by extinction procedures. *Journal of Abnormal Social Psychology, 59,* 269.

Wills, G., & Hall, R. V. (1974). A school counselor assists a teacher in reducing disruptions by a second grade girl. In R. V. Hall (Ed.), *Managing behavior: Part 3. Applications in school and home.* Austin, TX: PRO-ED.